Fun With Proverbs

Fun With Proverbs

John B. & Ching Yee Smithback

AN AUTHORS GUILD BACKINPRINT.COM EDITION

Fun With Proverbs

AN AUTHORS GUILD BACKINPRINT.COM EDITION

Published by iUniverse, Inc.

For information address:
iUniverse, Inc.
2021 Pine Lake Road, Suite 100
Lincoln, NE 68512
www.iuniverse.com

Originally published by Cove Press

First Edition

Illustrated by Ching Yee Smithback

ISBN-13: 978-0-595-35079-7
ISBN-10: 0-595-35079-8

Printed in the United States of America

Preface

A proverb is many things to many people. It may be defined as a wise old saying or as a short and frank expression. At other times, it is called a byword or a clever phrase of wisdom.

The terms 'succinct and 'pithy' often are used to describe a proverb, indicating the sayings are direct and to the point — while, at the same time, containing some helpful, practical or cautionary advice.

Perhaps it's best not to look so hard; let's say that a proverb is a phrase that expresses an idea, a caution, a judgment or an observation in a few short words. Proverbs also are phrases that stick in our minds and perform a valuable role by helping us to express ourselves.

As life changes, so do our proverbs. The wording of many of them has been modernized. **Least said, soonest mended** is one example that comes to mind, and it may not be realized that this is the same proverb as **least said, soonest forgotten**. The proverbs in this book are presented in their modern, up-to-date form.

And now, since **laughter is the best medicine**, begin reading and enjoying *Fun with Proverbs*!

ABSENCE MAKES THE HEART GROW FONDER

It's been a long time since I've seen a sight as sad as this! Timothy's worst enemy has gone on holiday—and Timothy misses him! Perhaps the saying **absence makes the heart grow fonder** is true after all. It says we miss someone or something more when we are away from it or don't have it.

ACTIONS SPEAK LOUDER THAN WORDS

I see Blah doesn't have the support of the audience," Calvin frowned. "The reason he is unpopular is because he promises much but delivers little. He's forgotten that **actions speak louder than words.**" In other words, what people do is more important than what they say they will do.

2

ADAM'S ALE/WINE

Ale is a strong beer, and Adam was the first man on earth. When Adam was thirsty, all he had to drink was water. From that, **Adam's ale** and **Adam's wine** are humorous ways of referring to the water we drink. "No coffee for me, thanks," Helen said. "I'll just have a glass of **Adam's ale.**"

ALL ROADS LEAD TO ROME

When the Roman Empire stretched across Europe, its engineers built roads which all led to Rome. "Like a spider web with Rome in the center," Teddy said. Teddy's right, and that has given us this saying that now means there are many different ways of attaining a single goal. "I may do things in an unusual way but **all roads lead to Rome,** and my methods seem to work."

4

ALL THAT GLITTERS IS NOT GOLD

On the occasion of his birthday, the King thought it would be nice to issue a gold coin. "Not of real gold, though," he advised. The treasury responded by distributing plastic coins. "They're lovely, and they'll remind everyone **all that glitters is not gold**," the King smiled. This means things don't have to be bright, beautiful or expensive to be of value.

ALL'S FISH THAT COMES TO THE NET

Fibb caught a mermaid. Forlornly, Fibb flung the mermaid back into the sea. Mrs. Fibb frowned. "But dear, isn't it true what fishermen say, that **all's fish that comes to the net**?" This proverb tells us that when something comes our way, we should consider how it might be used to benefit us.

AN APPLE A DAY KEEPS THE DOCTOR AWAY

If doctors had to depend on me to make a living, they'd be in financial trouble," Eve said. "Why is that?" her friend Adam asked. "Because I like apples," Eve smiled. I believe Eve is alluding to the saying **an apple a day keeps the doctor away**. It means that apples are so nutritious they keep you in the peak of health.

AN EXCEPTION
TO THE RULE

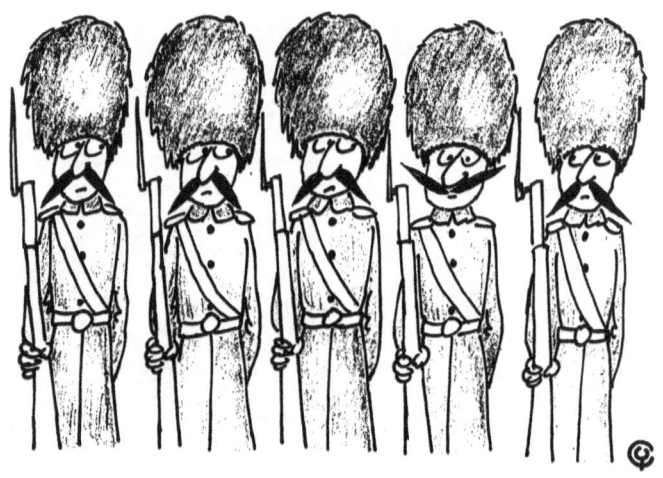

While inspecting his troops, the captain noticed something odd. "What's wrong with you?" he shouted at Wilburforce. "My moustache grows upward," Wilburforce replied. "In the army there are no **exceptions to the rule**," the captain barked—and no one saw Wilburforce again. **An exception to the rule** is something that does not conform to or agree with a rule.

AN OUNCE OF PREVENTION IS BETTER THAN A POUND OF CURE

The value of a cure for an illness can't be measured. This saying goes a step further and states that it is better to be cautious and prevent a misfortune or an accident from happening. "Be sure to get lots of exercise, and eat nutritious food to stay healthy. Remember that **an ounce of prevention is better than a pound of cure.**"

ANOTHER DAY, ANOTHER DOLLAR

THIS IS THE BEST PART OF THE DAY!

This particular remark can be heard at the end of a working day or at the conclusion of a job. People say it because they are pleased that their hard day is over and they have earned their pay. "Well, that's it," Eggmont sighed as the tourist boat faded into the sunset. "**Another day, another dollar.**" "You'd better mention that this is a North American expression," Petrock smiled.

AS A MAN MAKES HIS BED, SO MUST HE LIE IN IT

This proverb is of particular interest to Ahmed. "That's true," he responded, "for as you can see I am in the process of making my bed—and I am making it very carefully!" That's a good idea, for this tells us that when we do something or set out upon a particular course of action, we must accept the consequences of our actions. "Be they good or bad," Ahmed added.

AS I LIVE AND LEARN!

When he saw Granny going to school with the children, one of her neighbors was amazed. "Well, **as I live and learn!**" he exclaimed. Granny simply grinned. "We're never too old to learn," she said. **As I live and learn!** expresses surprise. It's used when one encounters a new experience or sees something very unusual.

A BAD WORKMAN
BLAMES HIS TOOLS

Incompetent people who do bad or careless work frequently blame their tools, material, equipment, working conditions–just about anything–for their failures or shortcomings. That's the idea behind this proverb. "That's an unusual apple you have painted, Robert." "It's strange because my brush is broken," he said. Robert sounds like **a bad workman blaming his tools**.

BE ON THE SAFE SIDE

It takes Arnie less than an hour to get to work, but to **be on the safe side** he leaves his house very early in the morning. "We live in uncertain times when anything might happen," Arnie said, "So to **be on the safe side,** I allow myself a couple of hours to get to the office." This expression means to take special precautions to avoid making a mistake.

BEAUTY IS IN THE EYE
OF THE BEHOLDER

Prunella is Robert's new model. "She's not exactly a beauty queen," he said, "but to me she's perfect." Prunella blushed. **"Beauty is in the eye of the beholder**, Robert." "Indeed it is," he replied, "and this old saying tells us that the idea of beauty exists in our minds. What is beautiful to one person may not be beautiful to others." That caused Prunella to blush again.

BEAUTY IS ONLY
SKIN DEEP

When something is skin deep, it is shallow and superficial. Therefore, to say that **beauty is only skin deep** implies that the beauty or appeal of something or someone doesn't extend very far. "Barbie seems like such an enchanting actress, but those who know her say that **beauty is only skin deep** because much of her appeal is owed to her fashionable clothes and makeup."

A BED OF ROSES

L ife," Chadwick grinned, "is **a bed of roses**." Then he frowned. "The only time it's not is when I'm called upon to chase mice. Not many people know this, but I really can't stand the things!" Then Chadwick yawned and went back to sleep. **A bed of roses** describes a life or a situation that is agreeable and gives comfort, peace and pleasure.

BEGGARS CAN'T BE CHOOSERS

Since Fergus is usually in need, he's the ideal person to explain this saying. "It says that someone in need should be grateful for what is given him—even if it's not what he wants or expects," he said. "Once I found a purse. I returned it to its owner, of course, and was given a dollar. It wasn't much, and I hoped for more; but when you're hungry, **beggars can't be choosers.**"

BETTER AN EGG TODAY
THAN A HEN
TOMORROW

If you want fresh eggs, you need a hen," Elmer said. "But then you'd have to get a young chick and raise it—and that takes time. So think of the proverb, **better an egg today than a hen tomorrow,** and buy my eggs now," he advised. "It's quicker—and besides, the chicken you raise yourself may turn out to be a rooster!"

BETTER LATE
THAN NEVER

Even if we do something late, it is better than not doing it at all. "That's what this proverb says," Orville said, "and I've been thinking about it for a long time. Maybe I should have asked Olivia to marry me when we were young," he said. Olivia, who had been waiting for Orville's proposal, smiled as they left the church. **"Better late than never,"** she said.

BIG FISH EAT
LITTLE FISH

This saying tells us that timid folks are easily overcome by those who are strong; that the weak will be subdued by those more aggressive. The idea extends through all areas of life—from school to business. "Down in the sea," said Annabelle Lee, "**big fish eat little fish** and life is a struggle." It's the same here on land, Annabelle!

(A) BIRD IN THE HAND IS WORTH TWO IN THE BUSH

"Some birds are worth more than others," Matilda said. "My little canary is priceless." Matilda's speaking about her pet bird, but that's not what is meant by **a bird in the hand is worth two in the bush**. It tells us that we should be satisfied with what we have and not risk losing it for something we imagine will be better. "That's why I'm happy with my canary—even though it doesn't sing," Matilda smiled.

BIRDS OF A FEATHER
FLOCK TOGETHER

Awwwk!

B irds of the same type always group
(flock) together. This saying means that
people who have things in common or
share the same interests usually gather
together. "The older girls won't play with
me," Betsy pouted. "They say, **birds of a
feather flock together** and I should play with
kids my own age."

BITE THE HAND THAT FEEDS ONE

When Spencer needed help, he turned to his friend Joseph for assistance. Joseph offered advice and helped Spencer find a job. In the course of time, Spencer became wealthy and important in the community, yet when Joseph needed help, Spencer ignored him. "I would suggest," a mutual friend said, "that Spencer is the type of person who **bites the hand that feeds him**." I'm sorry to say, I must agree.

24

A BLACK SHEEP

Once upon a time, black sheep were considered less valuable than white ones. That caused farmers to look upon them with dislike—and it has given us this remark which refers to a person in a family or community considered unsatisfactory or disgraceful. Whether or not he is, is purely subjective. "That's Edie, the **black sheep** in our family. She quit school to join the circus!"

THE BLIND LEADING
THE BLIND

Iknow absolutely nothing about physics. If you asked me to help you with your physics lessons, it would be a perfect example of **the blind leading the blind**. This expression is used in any situation in which a person helping or advising someone else knows as little about the subject as the person who is being advised.

BOYS WILL BE BOYS

"Listen to all that noise coming from the Men's Club," Helga frowned. "I know," Mary smiled. "As they say, **boys will be boys.**" This expression is used humorously— and sometimes sarcastically—to say that grown men frequently continue to act and play like small boys. That is, they act rough, tough, and somewhat noisy. "Whose turn to play marbles?" Mr. Jeffers asked.

BREAD IS THE
STAFF OF LIFE

Hurrying home to make his evening meal, Robert wasn't at all surprised to see a gentleman going in the opposite direction using a loaf of bread as a cane. "That's because it's **the staff of life**," Robert said. Robert is referring to the saying **bread is the staff of life**. In it, bread means food and staff is a metaphor for our need for food to live.

28

THE BUCK STOPS
HERE/WITH SOMEONE

S top!" Podunk shouted. "I'm the boss. No matter who goofed up on the job, I am responsible. **The buck stops here.**" The proverb Podunk is using means a final decision or total responsibility for an action rests with the speaker. In this case, **the buck stops with** Podunk.

BURN THE CANDLE AT BOTH ENDS

Those who are always busy and seem to get little rest are said to **burn the candle at both ends.** During examination time, Lily can be seen attending classes during the day and studying until the wee hours of the night. "I'll be happy when I graduate. I'll sleep all day and never have to **burn the candle at both ends** again," she daydreamed.

A BURNT CHILD
DREADS THE FIRE

We learn many things by experience and those that are painful are not quickly forgotten. That's the concept behind the proverb, **a burnt child dreads the fire**. It says that if we've been burnt, we will be more careful about a possible problem in the future.

BUY A PIG IN A POKE

Those who buy something without examining it for faults or checking to see if they received what they asked for are **buying a pig in a poke**. "What in the world is a poke?" Elmer asked. A poke is an old, old word for a sack or cloth bag. "So, if I bought Ed's old car without having a mechanic look at it, I'd be **buying a pig in a poke**?" That's right, Elmer.

CALL A SPADE A SPADE

When people **call a spade a spade,** they say exactly what they mean in clear, easy to understand language. They are direct, honest, and don't hide unpleasant facts or truths behind kind words. "I don't think I like you, Max," Maggie said in a frank, honest and straightforward manner. "Ah, but I like you very much because you always **call a spade a spade,**" Max blushed.

CAST PEARLS BEFORE SWINE

S wine are pigs, and to our knowledge, pigs have no great understanding of or appreciation for things of value. The meaning behind this saying (from the Bible) is a caution: be wary of giving something of value to those unable to appreciate it. "It was like **casting pearls before swine** to read my beautiful poems to that loud and unappreciative group," Byron sighed.

A CAT MAY LOOK
AT A KING

About 300 years ago this was a popular phrase in England. It meant that one person was no more important than another, and it was addressed to those who thought themselves superior to others. Today it's used to say, "I may not be important, but I have the same rights that you have!" "I may be new here, but so what? **A cat may look at a king**," Matilda said.

CATCH-AS-CATCH-CAN

O zzie can neither kick nor run, so there was no logical reason for putting him on our team," the coach said. "But we need a goalkeeper and Ozzie is the only one available. Giving him the position is more or less a case of **catch-as-catch-can**." I hope that doesn't offend Ozzie, because **catch-as-catch-can** means to do anything or use any means to achieve an aim or reach a goal.

CATCH YOUR BEAR
BEFORE YOU SELL
ITS SKIN

I don't suppose this ancient saying has much relevance in these modern times," Whoozit said. Marta smiled. "Have you seen the number of ladies waiting for winter coats over at Mr. Skinner's Emporium?" Actually, this tells us that we shouldn't be overly optimistic about something happening, and we should wait until it does happen before we act— or celebrate.

CATCH/CLUTCH/GRASP AT STRAWS

A drowning man will reach for anything to save himself, even pieces of straw. That's the idea behind this expression, which means to resort to any means to save oneself when in serious trouble. "The neighborhood kids must be desperate," Abe said. "How else can I explain the way they're **clutching at straws** to find ways to enjoy themselves?"

CHARITY BEGINS
AT HOME

This is a reminder that if one is to be kind
and generous, he should begin by first
taking care of himself and his family.
After that he can think of being charitable to
others. "Steven spends all his time helping
people, but he neglects his family. He must
remember that **charity begins at home.**"

CHILDREN SHOULD BE SEEN AND NOT HEARD

To the abiding sadness of children, this saying means exactly what the words say. Parents and adults use it to suggest that a child stop asking questions, talking, or making unnecessary noise. "You've been arguing too much," father said. "Haven't you heard that **children should be seen and not heard**?" "Isn't 'too much' a value judgment?" Dion whispered to her little brother.

CHRISTMAS COMES BUT ONCE EACH YEAR

Our ship's gone and we're stranded in the middle of the sea, but **Christmas comes but once each year** and I intend to celebrate!" Tim said. I wish Tim well—even though this saying is normally used to provide people with an excuse to indulge in food and drink and to spend money during the Christmas season.

CLEANLINESS IS NEXT TO GODLINESS

I'll just pop my little halo into this tub of soapy water and give it a good cleaning," Jamie smiled. "After all, **cleanliness is next to godliness**." What Jamie means is that to be clean and tidy is just as important as being spiritually good and righteous. "That's what I have been taught," Jamie proudly replied.

COUNT CHICKENS BEFORE THEY ARE HATCHED

Farmers know it's a mistake to have ten eggs and assume they will have ten chickens. Anyone who does would be **counting chickens before they are hatched.** This is usually expressed as a caution. "I may get promoted—but maybe I won't. I'll wait and see. I don't want to **count chickens before they're hatched.**"

CRY FOR THE MOON

If you have a dog, you might sometimes see it sitting outside staring up at the evening sky, **crying for the moon**. If that's the case, have a little compassion for the poor thing because when someone—or a dog—cries for the moon, he is making a request for something that is impossible to obtain. "I often think that my wish to have a world free of pollution is like **crying for the moon**," Agatha sighed.

CRY OVER SPILLED MILK

Natalie is a little girl with a big problem. The cow she was milking has overturned the milk pail. "I'm close to tears," Natalie cried. The cow is more relaxed about it. "A loss is a loss, but there's no point in **crying over spilled milk**." The cow's right—and this saying means it's pointless to get upset or feel regret about a loss or mistake that can't be undone.

CURIOSITY KILLED
THE CAT

Cats are said to have nine lives. It's also said that having too much curiosity kills them. That has given us this expression which we use to warn people not to show too much interest in affairs that don't concern them. "You attend to your affairs and I'll attend to mine. Remember that **curiosity killed the cat**."

CUT OFF ONE'S NOSE TO SPITE ONE'S FACE

When people are dissatisfied or angry, they sometimes react by doing foolish things that prove harmful to themselves. When someone does, he is said to **cut off his noise to spite his face.** "If you quit your job before you find another, you might be **cutting off your nose to spite your face,**" Tom cautioned his brother.

DAMNED IF ONE DOES, DAMNED IF ONE DOESN'T

I DID...
AND I DIDN'T...

Our football coach has a complaint: "No matter what decisions I make, there are always some people who will approve of them and some who won't," he said. "It's a case of **damned if I do, damned if I don't.**" The coach is saying that no matter what he does, someone is going to condemn or criticize him.

DEAD MEN TELL
NO TALES

This proverb states that those who are no longer alive aren't able to speak—and therefore won't reveal someone's deepest, darkest secrets. "We may never learn the truth behind the JFK assassination. All the witnesses are gone, and as you know, **dead men tell no tales.**"

THE DEVIL FINDS WORK
FOR IDLE HANDS

When Murice was young, his parents warned him that **the devil finds work for idle hands**. They were telling him that unless he kept busy doing useful and constructive things, he might be tempted into doing naughty things. "Yes, but I doubt that the proverb **the devil finds work for idle hands** means that I should waste my time sweeping floors!" Murice said to a stranger.

THE DEVIL HAS THE
BEST TUNES

Over 200 years ago, a religious leader in England named John Wesley turned popular songs of the day into church hymns. "Why should **the devil have the best tunes?**" he asked. Today someone doing unworthy things because it gives him pleasure might use this phrase humorously. "I know I watch too much television when I should be studying, but **the devil has the best tunes,**" Kurt said.

THE DEVIL IS NOT AS BLACK AS HE IS PAINTED

Robert fell asleep while painting someone's portrait. "It's time I taught this man a lesson," the devil said behind Robert's back. "Hasn't he heard, **the devil isn't as black as he is painted**?" I think Robert has heard the saying. It means, even a bad person possesses some good qualities.

THE DEVIL TAKE THE HINDMOST

I prefer the longer version of this proverb," Lucifer said. "And what is the longer rendition?" the donkey asked. "It is this: every man for himself, and **the devil take the hindmost**," Lucifer said. "And what does that mean?" the donkey inquired. "It means everyone should look after his own interests, with no regard to anyone else," Lucifer smiled. "I don't think I like that," the donkey replied.

DOG EAT DOG

In competitive situations where people have their own interests at heart and their own desires in mind, it is usually the strong and the determined who succeed. People refer to that type of situation as **dog eat dog**. "I'm happy that there's no **dog eat dog** in the office where I work," Mildred said. Millie is fortunate because there are some who might say we seem to live in a **dog-eat-dog** world.

DON'T CRY
STINKING FISH

A fish peddler wouldn't be successful if he told everyone that his fish were old and stinking. Like him, we should never bring someone's attention to our unfavorable qualities. On the contrary, we should always speak proudly of our best features, favorable qualities and exceptional abilities. "That's the real meaning behind **don't cry stinking fish,**" Jan said.

DON'T KILL THE GOOSE THAT LAYS THE GOLDEN EGGS

I read a story about a goose that laid golden eggs," Officer Mutt said. "Hoping to get all the eggs at once, the owner of the goose killed it. Frankly, I think it's a fable." Regardless of Mutt's beliefs, the fable has given us the proverb **don't kill the goose that lays the golden eggs**. "Meaning," Mutt said, "that we should not ruin or destroy something that benefits us or contributes to our success."

DON'T LOOK A GIFT HORSE IN THE MOUTH

Those who know about horses can estimate the age of one and learn its value by looking at its teeth. That has led to this proverb which says if someone gives you a gift or does you a favor, you should be grateful and not question it. In other words, **don't look a gift horse in the mouth** by wondering about its value or looking it over for faults.

DON'T PUT THE CART
BEFORE THE HORSE

Perrywinkle is confused. When he's
hooked to a wagon he's usually in front
and the wagon is behind. "Whoever did
this did it wrong," Perrywinkle frowned. "You
do not put the cart before the horse!"
Perrywinkle is alluding to a proverb that
means you should always do things in a
proper way and in the right order.

A DOSE OF ONE'S OWN MEDICINE

Medicine here refers to unfair, unjust, unpleasant or unsatisfactory treatment. When someone is given **a dose of his own medicine,** he receives the same bad treatment he has been handing out to someone else. "Hilton is always late," Sandra fumed. "I'm going to give him **a dose of his own medicine** and make him wait for me for a change!"

DRAW THE LINE

Sometimes we have to **draw the line** and say, "That's enough, that's as far as you can go." José wasn't happy that his brother always borrowed money and never repaid it. What José learned is that when we **draw the line**, we decide that there's a point beyond which we won't go—or allow others to go—if it makes us uncomfortable or unhappy. "No more loans," José told his brother.

THE EARLY BIRD
CATCHES THE WORM

Ever since I was a young chick, I've heard it said that **the early bird catches the worm**," Cyril sighed. "I get up early, but I never see any worms!" Someone should tell Cyril that this saying means that those who act more quickly than others are the ones most likely to achieve success or get what they want.

EAST OR WEST,
HOME IS THE BEST

Darting around in his speedy space ship, Esper has been to every corner of the cosmos. "I've been to places you folks haven't discovered," he said. But I'm sure Esper would agree that **east or west, home is the best**. "You're right. No matter where I go, I'm happiest when I'm at my home," he smiled.

EASY COME, EASY GO

Arnold is about to prove the truth of the saying, **easy come, easy go**. He found some money and he is about to spend it foolishly. "Oh, well," he sighed. **"Easy come, easy go."** This saying can refer to anything that is easily or quickly gained—and just as easily or quickly lost.

EVERY CLOUD HAS A
SILVER LINING

A drop of rain landed on Felix's head. That caused him to look up until he located a particular cloud. "Sometimes when it's raining we can see the sun peeking through the clouds," he said. "That causes some clouds to have a silver edge and has led to the saying that no matter how dark things are, **every cloud has a silver lining**." He smiled. "That means good things usually follow the bad."

EVERY DOG HAS
HIS DAY

B right Eyes had a period of bad luck. "It's the same with people," he said. "They have their bad times, too." Sure, but eventually the most unfortunate person or dog has a day in which he or she finds something to cheer about. "That's the meaning behind this," Bright Eyes smiled. "So when things are bad, don't be discouraged. Sooner or later, **every dog has his day.**"

EVERY LAW HAS
A LOOPHOLE

A loophole is a small opening. In law it refers to a way out of a penalty. It's usually because whoever wrote a particular law failed to write it carefully enough, and to take all things into consideration. "How could they have guessed that Albert would know the proverb **every law has a loophole**, and that he'd use every one of them to avoid punishment?" Mutt sighed.

EVERY PICTURE TELLS A STORY

A photograph often tells more about something than a written account of it. In the same way, this proverb says that someone's looks or acts reveal a great deal about him or her. "Polly's really happy. I can tell that by looking at her," Noel smiled. "Isn't it said, **every picture tells a story?**"

EXPERIENCE IS THE
BEST TEACHER

You can tell people how to do something, and you can show them how to do it, but most people will learn best if they do it themselves. Agatha's niece is just learning to fly her broom. "Hold tight and keep trying," Agatha smiled as her niece flew by. **"Experience is the best teacher."**

FAINT HEART NEVER
WON FAIR LADY

"There's a wonderful old saying that is worth remembering," Acton said to Newton. "I know you admire Gertie, but if you want to win her heart, remember that **faint heart never won fair lady**. That means you must be confident and strong to impress her," he said. Newton put on a mask and handed Gertie a flower. **"Faint heart never won fair lady,"** Gertie called as he ran away.

FALL BETWEEN TWO STOOLS

Hal's a disorganized writer and the result is that his work seems to **fall between two stools**. Things that **fall between two stools** are neither one thing nor another. For example, here's what the critics say about Hal's new book: "Hal has tried to present a serious story in a humorous way. Unfortunately, it **falls between two stools**, for it's neither serious nor funny." Poor Hal!

THE FAT IS IN THE FIRE

Don't put fat near an open flame! It's risky because it ignites easily and can lead to a fire. That's the idea behind this expression which says someone has done something that will lead to serious trouble. "Fergus and Buddy are thinking of a hot chicken dinner, but I'm afraid **the fat is in the fire!** Here come the farmers who own the chicken!"

FEED A COLD AND STARVE A FEVER

My mother and grandmother believed that the best way to treat an illness was as follows," Granny said. "If you have a cold, eat lots of food. If you have a fever, eat nothing. There's even a proverb to help you remember this," she added. "The proverb is: **Feed a cold and starve a fever.**"

FIDDLE WHILE ROME BURNS

In this proverb the word fiddle means to do nothing, and the origin of it goes back to 64 A.D. when it is said that Emperor Nero stood aside and played his fiddle while Rome was being destroyed in a horrible fire. The tale may not be true, but this remark has come to mean to do nothing while something serious is happening. "I **fiddled while Rome burned**," explained John. "I didn't study, and consequently failed my examinations."

73

FLING/SLING/THROW MUD AT SOMEONE

Fling, sling and throw mean nearly the same thing. In this proverb, to **fling, sling, or throw mud at someone** is to say evil or bad things about that person—and in doing so, to damage his or her reputation. "Some people **sling mud at people** just because they're jealous," Sammy said. "That's awful, isn't it?" It is—and wouldn't it be a nicer world if everyone stopped **throwing mud**?

74

FLOG/BEAT
A DEAD HORSE

To flog is to beat, and this particular remark is used figuratively to mean either to persist in pursuing a matter no one is interested in; or continuing to do something when no results can be achieved. "I often think trying to get people interested in conservation is like **flogging a dead horse**," declared an exasperated Roger.

A FOOL AND HIS MONEY ARE SOON PARTED

Many people know this proverb but few actually practice it. It says that a person who spends his money foolishly will soon be penniless. That is, he and his money are parted. "Rodney made a lot of money last month, but he spent it unwisely. **A fool and his money are soon parted**, they say."

FORGIVE AND FORGET

Officer Mutt caught Albert in the act of leaving his jail. "I was just stepping out for a pizza. **Forgive** me **and forget** it," Albert said. Mutt was furious. "You do such naughty things! How can you expect me to **forgive and forget!**" This expression refers to excusing or pardoning someone for doing something. "And then trying one's best to forget it!" Mutt muttered.

FRESH FIELDS AND PASTURES NEW

Expressions and proverbs come from many sources, and this one is from the poem *Lycidas*, written 350 years ago by John Milton. It refers to something new—as a job or hobby—or traveling to a new place. "Sometimes I'm like my cows and have a desire for **fresh fields and pastures new**," Mortimer said.

A FRIEND IN NEED IS A FRIEND INDEED

This saying—often shortened to **a friend in need**—describes a truly genuine friend. No matter how difficult things are for you, he or she can always be depended on to stand by you. Felix has several such friends. "Hey, you forgot your umbrella," both Herb and Hal called. "Take one of ours!" Felix smiled. **"A friend in need is a friend indeed,"** he said.

THE GAME IS NOT
WORTH THE CANDLE

It wasn't long ago that people relied on candles for light at night. When playing a game by the light of a candle, if it seemed a waste of time, they'd say **the game is not worth the candle**. Today, this expression is used to describe an activity or project that doesn't seem worth the time or effort spent on it. "That's interesting," Buddy grinned. "Whose turn is it to deal?"

GENIUS IS AN INFINITE CAPACITY FOR TAKING PAINS

The writer Thomas Carlyle said that genius consists of having limitless patience to do a perfect job—but he said it in the way it appears above. If someone were to ask me to give an example, I'd suggest they stand at Robert's window watching him work. "It's not easy painting butterflies!" Robert exclaimed.

GIVE SOMEONE ENOUGH ROPE AND HE WILL HANG HIMSELF

If encouraged, a person doing wrong, foolish or ridiculous things will keep on doing them. "He doesn't even have to be encouraged," Lester said. "Just let him keep doing wrong, because if you **give him enough rope, he'll hang himself**." What Lester means is that if we allow someone to continue in his bad ways, he'll eventually bring about his own downfall or ruin.

GIVE THE DEVIL HIS DUE

What is Felix doing? Why is he being so courteous and showing such respect to someone he absolutely despises? "Don't worry, I'm just **giving the devil his due**," Felix explained. Well, in this case we must admit that Felix is being very fair, for when we **give the devil his due**, we praise someone for his or her achievements—no matter how much we dislike or resent that person.

THE GODS SEND NUTS TO THOSE WHO HAVE NO TEETH

In this illustration, we see a group of elderly gentlemen looking out of the window during a most unusual storm. It is, in fact, raining walnuts, and the gentlemen are thinking that things in life are strange: we either have too little of what we want, or **the gods send nuts to those who have no teeth** and we have too much of what we cannot use.

A GOLDEN KEY OPENS EVERY DOOR

L ook what I found!" Albert cried. "Why,
it's a golden key!" Officer Mutt observed.
"It reminds me that **a golden key opens
every door**," Albert smiled. "Yes, I think it will
open a door for you at my nice jail," Mutt
replied. Actually, the golden key here refers to
money—and it is assumed it will let someone
do anything he or she wants to do.

GREAT MINDS
THINK ALIKE

If I have an idea, come to a conclusion or reach a decision about something that is the same as your idea, conclusion or decision, I might flatter both of us by saying, **"Great minds think alike!"** This is a humorous saying that suggests that we're both very clever and intelligent people.

GREENER PASTURES

I've discovered a way to keep my pastures looking fresh," Mortimer grinned, "and by offering my cows **greener pastures** they're happy to stay at home." **Greener pastures** refers to a place where conditions appear to be better or more livable. "My cows have gone to find **greener pastures**," one of Mortimer's neighbors complained. "That's how it is with cows," Mortimer replied. "They've probably moved on to **greener pastures**."

GRIN AND BEAR IT

FUN, ISN'T IT!

Skiing down a mountain, Chuck collided with a bear and got trapped beneath it. Known for his cheerful disposition, Chuck wasn't alarmed. "I have a way of looking at misfortune," he said. "I simply **grin and bear it**." To **grin and bear** it is to put up with discomfort or a bad situation without complaining. So Chuck's still there, **grinning and bearing it** while waiting for help to arrive.

88

HALF A LOAF IS BETTER THAN NONE

There is great meaning in the proverb, **half a loaf is better than none**," Buddy said. "On the surface, it says that we should consider ourselves lucky to have what we have. Beneath the surface, it tells us that if we receive less than we desire, we should be content and not yearn for more." With that, Buddy began to eat the bread that Robert had given him.

HALF THE WORLD
KNOWS NOT HOW THE
OTHER HALF LIVES

Most people in Egypt probably have no idea how the people in Canada or China live. This is generally true of folks everywhere, but this proverb usually refers to people from different economic positions as well as from different cultures or backgrounds. "Richard does not know what it is to be poor. Meanwhile, his neighbor John has nothing and is absolutely convinced that **half the world does not know how the other half lives**," Melissa said.

HARP ON ONE STRING

The harp is a musical instrument with many strings. "I wish someone would tell Doris that," Jennifer said. "It's getting awfully dull listening to her **harp on one string** all the time. All she ever talks about is her boyfriend, her boyfriend, her boyfriend!" When someone is accused of **harping on one string,** he or she speaks or writes about one subject. "Until it becomes boring," Jennifer added.

HAVE MORE THAN ONE STRING TO ONE'S BOW

People who hunt with bows and arrows carry a spare string in case the one in their bow breaks. That precaution has given us this British saying. It means we should have an option in case one idea or plan fails. "I wanted to be a sailor, but knowing it's wise to **have more than one string to my bow,** I became a doctor," Jessie said.

HAVE TWO BITES
AT THE CHERRY

Cherries aren't very big, so if we can't finish eating one with a single bite, we can usually finish it with two. From that idea comes this proverb (mostly British) which means to have a second opportunity to do something. "I failed my history quiz, but the teacher said she'd let me **have two bites at the cherry** and allow me to take it again."

HE THAT SUPS WITH THE DEVIL MUST HAVE A LONG SPOON

BON APPÉTIT !

The word sup means 'to eat,' and this proverb can be put in a more modern way by saying that those who deal with evil people should beware: they could become controlled or influenced by them. "I hope you are cautious when dealing with suspicious individuals," Babbit's mother told her son. **"He that sups with the devil must have a long spoon,"** she added.

HE WHO PAYS THE PIPER CALLS THE TUNES

The meaning behind this saying is that the person who pays for something has the right to do as he wants. That is, he can call the tunes. "It's my party, so I can invite anyone I want. After all, **he who pays the piper calls the tunes**," Cleo said.

A HEAVY PURSE MAKES A LIGHT HEART

The king sleeps well and has many pleasing dreams. "There's a reason for it," he explained. "To quote a proverb, **a heavy purse makes a light heart**." He paused. "It's such a nice saying, I don't know why everyone doesn't sleep well at night." It's probably because this means when one has lots of money, it makes him feel very happy!

HITCH ONE'S WAGON
TO A STAR

Many years ago travelers used the stars to guide them in the correct direction over land and sea. That led to this proverb which means to move forward in a way to improve one's chances of achieving success. "I have a goal in life," Teddy said, "and to accomplish it I'm going to **hitch my wagon to a star** and spend more time in the library studying my lessons."

HOME IS WHERE THE HEART IS

No matter where anyone is, home is where people feel most comfortable and content. It is where they really and truly want to be. "No matter where my steps might lead me, my heart will always be here with you and my good friends," Albert said. "I know," Officer Mutt said. "**Home is where the heart is.**"

IDLE FOLK HAVE THE LEAST LEISURE

Winsome weaves throughout the day, while Hiznibs sleeps the day away. When he's asked to work, he says, "I'm busy." But Winsome works until she's dizzy. "I'm demonstrating that **idle folk have the least leisure**," Hiznibs yawned, "a saying that means those who work hard to avoid work have little time left to do any work."

IF IT'S NOT ONE THING IT'S ANOTHER

I wonder why it is that when we have a problem or experience difficulties, our troubles and problems always seem to multiply? "I have often wondered about that myself," Albert frowned. "In fact, I have often said to myself, **if it's not one thing it's another**." Like Albert, we use this expression when our woes seem to go on and on without end.

IF MONEY BE NOT THY SERVANT IT WILL BE THY MASTER

This proverb—and you are likely to see a number of variations of it—is a caution: use money wisely and you are its master. Use it badly and you become its slave. No one knows better than the King, for he has this to say about it: **"Money hasn't made me its servant** for I'm the humble master of all the money I collect from my subjects!"

IF PIGS COULD FLY

O nce upon a time someone suggested
that I couldn't fly," Gordo grinned.
"They were so certain that they created
the cynical remark, **if pigs could fly.** What
they were saying was that **if pigs could fly,**
then any manner of strange and miraculous
things were possible." Example: "**If pigs
could fly,** we'd all be millionaires."

IF THE HAT/SHOE FITS, WEAR IT

If something unpleasant is said about someone which could apply to you, you should take notice of it. If necessary, you should accept it as constructive criticism. That's what we mean when we say **if the shoe fits, wear it**. "I didn't say you look funny, but if the hat fits, wear it!"

IF WISHES WERE HORSES, BEGGARS WOULD RIDE

If we could get all the things we wanted just by making a wish, we would have all we ever wanted. That would include beggars, of course, who could suddenly become rich by wishing for gold. **"If wishes were horses, beggars would ride** and I'd live in a big house."

IF YOU CAN'T BITE, DON'T SHOW YOUR TEETH

I just heard a funny proverb, Timothy laughed. "Which one?" See-Saw asked. **"If you can't bite, don't show your teeth!"** Timothy exclaimed. "It says if you have a complaint but can't do anything about it except shout, you should remain silent." That made See-Saw laugh so much he began to bark. Then his dentures fell out.

IF YOU CAN'T LICK THEM, JOIN THEM

So many of our friends have moved away," Lily said. "Most have run off to join the circus," Leslie added. At that very moment they saw Louis going by in a cage. **"If you can't lick them, join them,"** he advised. Louis was quoting a proverb which is defined like this: if you cannot defeat an opponent or get him to change his ideas, plans or ways, the best thing to do is to change your ideas, plans or ways and join him.

IF YOU SCRATCH MY BACK, I'LL SCRATCH YOURS

Don't take this expression literally, for it has nothing to do with scratching or backs. It means, if you help me, I'll help you. It can also be changed to, **I'll scratch your back if you scratch mine.** "I need help repairing my house," Manny said. **"If you scratch my back, I'll scratch yours,"** he promised.

IN FOR A PENNY, IN FOR A DOLLAR/POUND

The pound here is the British pound sterling. A penny is 1/100 part of one. This old saying tells us that if we decide to do something, we should commit ourselves to it boldly and completely. "I'm going to devote myself to earning as much as possible this summer," Teddy said. "After all, **in for a penny, in for a dollar**."

IN THE LAND OF THE BLIND, THE ONE-EYED MAN IS KING

Some proverbs are direct and to the point. Others present an idea in an abstract way—like this one which says that someone with only limited ability or talent has an advantage over those with none. "Knute has been promoted because he's the only one here who carries a big stick. **In the land of the blind, the one-eyed man is king,**" Toby said.

IT SHOULDN'T HAPPEN TO A DOG

O nce upon a time dogs were treated quite badly. "That's the reason for this saying," Bolivar said, hobbling along. Today we use the expression to complain about a terrible experience or when things are going badly for us. "I know. I've just had one of those days when everything went wrong and nothing went right. **It shouldn't happen to a dog,**" Bolivar sighed.

IT TAKES A THIEF TO CATCH A THIEF

The best way to catch a thief or a dishonest person is to trap him by using his own methods. I heard an example of that the other day when it was reported that Officer Mutt had sent someone to catch a robber in the park. "It was easy," Mutt declared. "As you know, **it takes a thief to catch a thief**. So I sent Albert, a convicted thief, to catch a thief."

IT TAKES TWO TO MAKE A QUARREL

M ost of us would find it impossible to
have an argument with ourselves
because **it takes two to make a
quarrel**. "Who says it's impossible? I argue
with myself every day!" Filibuster said. I'm
glad everyone isn't like Filibuster. This
proverb tells us that there wouldn't be a
quarrel if one party refused to participate in an
argument. Similarly, it takes two to tango.

IT'S A SMALL WORLD

Hey, look at that foot! It looks familiar, doesn't it?" Zeke shouted. "It sure does," Oliver replied. "I saw it when we lived in Zanesville. **It's a small world**, isn't it?" It certainly is, and the phrase Oliver hurriedly uttered is used to express surprise when seeing someone or something from the past. "Like the bottom of a big foot," Oliver added.

IT'S LOVE THAT MAKES THE WORLD GO 'ROUND/AROUND

When people are in love, the world appears to be a happier and more wonderful place where joy is found in the smallest things. It is to lovers, then, that we owe this saying, for **it's love that makes the world go 'round/around**. That is, love makes this old world of ours a better place in which to live.

JAM TOMORROW

I n *Alice Through the Looking Glass*, The White
Queen offers Alice a job saying, "I'll give
you **jam tomorrow and jam yesterday—
but never jam today.**" Shortened to **jam
tomorrow**, the expression now refers to a
time in the future when better things are
promised. "During an election year everything
is **jam tomorrow**. People will say anything to
get elected!"

A JOB WORTH DOING
IS A JOB WORTH
DOING WELL

Jeffery has made what may be his last great trip of exploration. Watching someone trying to build a fire by rubbing sticks together, he became distressed. "Haven't you heard that **a job worth doing is a job worth doing well**? Here, use my lighter!" This proverb means when one does something he should do it as well as he can.

KEEP A DOG AND
BARK ONESELF

P eople who keep a dog to guard their
property would be very unhappy if the
dog failed to do his duty. In the same
way, a boss who has to do work her employees
should be doing might complain to them by
using this expression: "You're never around
when I need you! I might as well **keep a dog
and bark myself!**"

KEEP THE WOLF FROM THE DOOR

Wolves, it is said, prey on the weak when searching for food. Thus, the 'wolf' in this expression is a metaphor for hunger. To **keep the wolf from the door**, then, is to avoid hunger and poverty. "I don't like my job," Rudolph confessed, "But I have to do something to **keep the wolf from the door**."

KILL TWO BIRDS WITH ONE STONE

W hen someone **kills two birds with one stone,** two things are accomplished by performing one action. For example, one of the birds in this illustration is saying to the other: "Why don't we **kill two birds with one stone** by stopping off to visit Aunt Martha when we fly south this winter?"

KNOW A HAWK FROM A HANDSAW

When Shakespeare was searching for a way to have Hamlet tell people that he was no fool and knew exactly what he was talking about, he gave Hamlet these words to say. Lo and behold, here is Teddy using the same words to describe his uncle! "That's right. He's the smartest man in the world. If anyone **knows a hawk from a handsaw**, Uncle Felix does," Teddy proclaimed.

LAUGH AND THE WORLD LAUGHS WITH YOU

Most people like to laugh. I guess that's why someone once said that laughter is contagious. Therefore, people like being with someone who is in a happy, cheerful mood. That's the meaning behind **laugh and the world laughs with you**. The complete saying is this: **laugh and the world laughs with you, weep and you weep alone.**

LAUGHTER IS THE BEST MEDICINE

There's an old saying that tells us that if we stay cheerful and keep laughing, we'll quickly forget all our troubles. So whenever you are sad, tell yourself that **laughter is the best medicine.** "And don't forget to wear a big smile," Dr. Huang instructed me.

LEAST SAID, SOONEST FORGOTTEN

After making a mistake, saying or doing the wrong thing, or perhaps embarrassing ourselves or others in some way, we tend to think and worry about it—and we might apologize for it over and over. Usually, **least said, soonest forgotten**. That is, the less we say about it, the sooner the incident will be forgotten.

LEAVE/LET WELL ENOUGH ALONE

When George finished his sculpture, he stopped working on it. A friend suggested he change the body, but George wisely said, "No, **leave well enough alone**. The sculpture is fine as is." To **leave/let well enough alone** is to ignore or disregard something or someone when making a change might be too problematic or challenging. That's exactly what George is doing.

A LEOPARD CAN'T
CHANGE HIS SPOTS

This is a figurative way of saying that it's impossible for someone to change his basic nature," Robert explained. "He is what he is—and there's nothing he can do about it. It's an expression that appears in the Bible." Even as he speaks, Robert seems intent on seeing what he can do to help **a leopard change his spots**. "I'm experimenting," he said.

LET SLEEPING DOGS LIE

It has been said that a sleeping dog shouldn't be disturbed, for if it were suddenly awakened it might cause trouble. That has given us this proverb, a metaphor, which means there are some topics we shouldn't mention if talking about them makes someone uncomfortable. "I don't want to hear how my watchdog slept through last night's burglary! Forget it and **let sleeping dogs lie!**" Andy exclaimed.

LIFE IS JUST A BOWL
OF CHERRIES

T his is the title of a song that was popular
in the U.S. in the 1930's. The song spoke
of life being full of happiness and
pleasure—though there was a certain amount
of sarcasm in it. Today the expression might
be used hopefully—or mockingly. "I just got
promoted! **Life is just a bowl of cherries!**" "I
feel terrible, but I keep telling myself that **life
is just a bowl of cherries.**"

LIGHT NOT A CANDLE
TO THE SUN

Gully is attracted to rocks. "Whenever I see one, I have an irresistible urge to paint it," he said. "Gee, Gully, you're a genius!" Gertie grinned. Gully was grim. **"Light not a candle to the sun,"** he replied. That silenced Gertie, for this proverb says that one should not stress the obvious.

LIGHTNING NEVER STRIKES TWICE

There's an old saying that lightning never strikes in the same place twice. That's usually shortened to **lightning never strikes twice**. It means that the same thing is not likely to occur to someone more than once. "If you've been offered a big promotion, accept it. After all, **lightning never strikes twice**."

LIKE A BULL IN A CHINA SHOP

I magine how this place would look if a bull
came in that door," someone said to Felix.
"Then we'd see what people mean when
they say, **like a bull in a china shop!**" Felix
had a bad dream about that, but he woke up
remembering that someone described as being
like a bull in a china shop is a clumsy, tactless
person. "And he's sure to create a mess!"
Felix said.

LIKE LOOKING FOR A NEEDLE IN A HAYSTACK

Looking for a lost needle in a pile of hay (a haystack) can be an almost impossible task. From that, when something is very hard to find, we say it's **like looking for a needle in a haystack**. "Trying to find a quiet place to study is **like looking for a needle in a haystack**," Teddy said.

LITTLE PITCHERS HAVE BIG EARS

The word pitcher sounds like the word picture—so I guess Robert got confused when he heard someone say, "**Little pitchers have big ears.**" In this saying, a 'pitcher' is a curious child, and the pitcher's handles are the child's 'big ears.' Parents often say this to warn someone that a child is listening in on their private conversation. "We shouldn't discuss that in front of the children. **Little pitchers have big ears.**"

LOCK THE STABLE DOOR
AFTER THE HORSE
HAS BOLTED

Once a mistake has been made or an error committed, it's too late to take precautions to prevent it from happening. Therefore, we should take care to prevent trouble before—not after—it happens. "That's why I'm locking up," Mortimer said. "It does no good to **lock the stable door after the horse has bolted.**"

THE LONGEST DAY
MUST HAVE AN END

Some days seem particularly long and endless, especially when we're unhappy. Every day does end, though, even those that are painful or difficult. By extension, all difficult jobs or situations also have an end. "This has been an awful day," Felix mumbled, "but even **the longest day must have an end**, thank goodness!"

LOOK BEFORE
YOU LEAP

"I never make mistakes," Henry declared. "I always **look before I leap**." His wife wasn't so sure of that. "How about the time you jumped into the lake?" she asked. "Oh, that was different," Henry smiled. "I was so overcome with love for you that I wasn't thinking clearly at the time." In truth, to **look before you leap** means to give careful consideration to your actions before you perform them.

LOOK ON THE BRIGHT/SUNNY SIDE

You've been looking a little sad lately, so I painted this elegant picture for you," Officer Mutt said. Albert gazed at it. "It looks sunny and bright—what is it?" "That's the idea, it's something to remind you to **look on the bright side**," Mutt answered. To **look on the bright or sunny side** is to be hopeful and see the good—not the bad—in any situation.

LOSERS WEEPERS,
FINDERS KEEPERS

This is an old rhyming statement used mostly by children. If someone loses something, he weeps—but if someone finds it, he keeps it. As you might imagine, children who say this are usually "the finders" of something. "The King can't find his crown. **Losers weepers, finders keepers,**" Nobbin laughed.

LOVE IS BLIND

According to this old saying, a person in love doesn't see—or at least admit to seeing—faults in the person he or she loves. Herbie, for example, thinks Maggie is the sweetest and dearest girl on the face of the planet Earth. "If Herbie believes **love is blind**, it's probably my fault," Cupid said. "I'm experimenting to see if I can hit anything with a blindfold on."

LOVE ME, LOVE MY DOG

This old saying comes from the fact that people who have dogs expect others to appreciate them as much as they do. It has come to mean that if we want a person's friendship we must totally accept him or her, faults and all. "I know I talk too much, Harry, but as the saying goes, **love me, love my dog**."

MAKE HAY WHILE THE SUN SHINES

Farmers with hay to harvest don't wait until it's raining to go to their fields—they take advantage of bright, sunny days. From that, **make hay while the sun shines** refers to taking advantage of a favorable situation to benefit or profit from it. "Everyone has gone to bed, so I'm going to **make hay while the sun shines** and finish my book while it's quiet," Sarah said.

MAKE A MOUNTAIN OUT OF A MOLEHILL

Moles are tiny creatures that live beneath the soil. They're known for digging small—but annoying—hills called molehills. People who exaggerate a problem or a worry that isn't very important **make a mountain out of a molehill.** "Teddy's very calm. He's not the type to ever **make a mountain out of a molehill.**"

MAN DOES NOT LIVE BY BREAD ALONE

I t's a known fact that **man does not live by bread alone**," Robert said. "That's the reason I'm adding a jar of jam and a pot of honey to my latest painting." The expression Robert is referring to comes from the Bible, and it says a person's spiritual needs are just as important to his well-being as the needs of his body. "I'll make this plum jam," Robert said.

MANNERS MAKE
THE MAN

At first glance you wouldn't know that Fergus is a perfect gentleman. But according to this saying, a man's true character is revealed by the way he conducts himself, not by the way he looks. Just how polite he is will tell you a lot about him. "Oh, sir, you have shown me that it is true, **manners make the man**," Miss Dimples smiled.

MANY HANDS MAKE LIGHT WORK

Mr. Hayday is fortunate to have found someone as useful as Ollie for his shipping department. Not only does Ollie do the work of several people, he sings songs while he works. "Two hands good, eight hands better," he sings. Ollie is good— and he's proving the saying that **many hands** (people) sharing a job or task **make light** (easier) **work** of it.

MARCH COMES IN LIKE A LION AND GOES OUT LIKE A LAMB

In old English, March was named The Stormy Month. The French called it The Windy Month. Named after the Roman god of war, March has a reputation of beginning with wild storms and ending peacefully with the arrival of spring. "Don't worry," said Peter during the rain storm, **"March comes in like a lion and goes out like a lamb."**

MARRIAGES ARE MADE IN HEAVEN

"People often say that **marriages are made in heaven**," Polly said. "What does that mean?" Don asked. "It means that long before we met, it was decided in heaven that we were ideally suited for each other, and that we would one day meet and get married," Polly smiled. "She's absolutely right," Jamie grinned. "That's what keeps us so busy here."

MIGHT AS WELL BE HUNG FOR A SHEEP AS A LAMB

Long ago in England, a person could be hung for stealing a sheep. A lamb is a baby sheep and much smaller, but the penalty was the same for stealing either. Therefore, this proverb says if a person is going to do something that will be met with disapproval he might as well do something that will please or benefit him.

MONEY BURNS A HOLE IN SOMEONE'S POCKET

Here is a riddle: What is it that some people are so eager to get rid of, that it seems to **burn a hole in their pocket** and disappear? The answer is money. "No sooner do the workers get their wages, but the **money** seems to **burn a hole in their pockets** and they rush out to spend it," Basil commented.

MONEY CAN'T BUY
EVERYTHING

Some people think if they have enough money they can buy anything. They should be careful, though, and remember the old saying, **money can't buy everything.** "Health and happiness are two excellent examples of things that aren't for sale," Pierre declared, "and our beautiful monuments aren't available, either!"

MONEY DOESN'T GROW
ON TREES

It's difficult for children to understand that
money doesn't grow on trees. That is,
money isn't as abundant as leaves and it
certainly doesn't fall from the skies. This old
saying is meant to advise us that we should
spend our money carefully because work is
required to earn it.

MONEY IS THE ROOT
OF ALL EVIL

I wonder if it's really true that **money is the root of all evil**," Teddy pondered. In the Bible it says that it is. It says (1 Timothy 6:10) that the love of **money is the root of all evil**. "Maybe if I didn't actually love it, but just sort of enjoyed it a little bit, that would be okay," Teddy said.

MONEY TALKS

The saying **money talks** refers to the fact that people who have a lot of money generally find it much easier to gain favors and advantages than people who are poor. "My rich aunt never has to wait for a table when she goes to a restaurant. As the saying goes, **money talks**."

THE MOUNTAIN ISN'T GOING TO COME TO MOHAMMED

This is a reminder that if you want something, it's not going to come about by itself. You must take action to attain your goals. "If it's success you're after, you'll have to work for it. Keep in mind that **the mountain isn't going to come to Mohammed**," Mrs. Bell said to her son Alexander.

THE MOUNTAIN LABORS AND BRINGS FORTH A MOUSE

BECAUSE IT'S THERE !

WHY?

What's that funny statue doing there?" Bimbi asked. "It's there to encourage someone to think up a silly saying," Hoozit said. In time, someone proved Hoozit correct by creating the above proverb. Hoozit even knew what it would mean: to work hard and long on a project that turns out to be pretty useless.

MY HOME IS MY CASTLE

Our laws guarantee absolute privacy in our homes: we can close the doors and no one can enter without permission. That leads us to feel that our homes are our personal castles—and that's the story behind this British saying. "I wonder if people in other countries think as we do, that **my home is my castle**?" Winston wondered.

NECESSITY IS THE
MOTHER OF INVENTION

People don't invent things that aren't essential or useful, they invent them because they are necessary. "I had trouble seeing in the dark," Thomas Edison explained, "so I invented the light bulb. **Necessity is the mother of invention.**"

NEVER SAY DIE

I visited a place in my dreams," Ken said, "where a pleasing voice said he had been watching me from afar and admired me because I **never say die!**" Ken should accept that as a compliment for the saying **never say die** encourages someone to have faith, show courage, keep trying, and never give up.

A NEW BROOM
SWEEPS CLEAN

Someone new to a position of responsibility usually views matters in a different way and is quick to make changes. "Especially to try to improve things," Agatha smiled. Such a person is called a new broom, a title borrowed from the proverb **a new broom sweeps clean**. "That's why the boss hired me," Agatha said, "because no one knows more about brooms than I do!"

NO NEWS IS
GOOD NEWS

If something good happens, we seldom
hear about it. If something bad happens,
we hear about it immediately. It's on
television, in the newspapers, it's everywhere.
For that reason, we've come to believe that if
we hear no news about something it's because
it's good news. "I've given up reading or
listening to the daily news," Felix said. "**No
news is good news.**"

NOT FOR ALL THE COFFEE IN BRAZIL

I will gladly trade you my bags of coffee for your very appealing box of tea," Carlos smiled. "No, no, a thousand times no!" Ah-Jon replied. "I am not interested. I will not trade you my box of tea, **not for all the coffee in Brazil!**" Well, that's that, for to say **not for all the coffee in Brazil** means absolutely, positively, definitely not!

NOT FOR ALL THE TEA
IN CHINA

How much tea is there in China? "Oh, there's lots and lots, tons and tons," Ah-Jon replied. "But that's not enough," Sik Yee said, "for you have asked me for my hand, but I shall not marry you. **Not for all the tea in China!**" That will disappoint Ah-Jon, because **not for all the tea in China** means absolutely, positively and definitely not!

NOT THE ONLY PEBBLE
ON THE BEACH

 eggy and Polly had a quarrel. "I'll never
talk to you again!" Peggy shouted.
 "What do I care? You're **not the only
pebble on the beach**," Polly answered. I hope
these two settle their dispute soon because
when someone uses this expression, he or she
is boldly saying, "You're not the only person in
the world!"

ON A/ONE'S HIGH HORSE

LUCKY I DON'T HAVE ACROPHOBIA!

Someone **on a high horse** can be difficult to deal with. "There's an explanation for that," Hallaway said, "because someone **on a high horse** is haughty and proud—and he may think he's better than anyone around him." Hallaway should know; he's been **on his high horse** ever since he got promoted. "Yes, I'm the boss of the riding club now," Hallaway declared.

ONCE BITTEN, TWICE SHY

Ned's dog hasn't shown much interest in playing with him lately. **"Once bitten, twice shy,"** the dog whimpered. This says if you have had a bad experience doing something (**once bitten**) you will be extremely reluctant (**twice shy**) about repeating the mistake. "The last time I played with Ned he bit me! That kid's rough!" the dog explained.

ONE MAN'S MEAT
IS ANOTHER
MAN'S POISON

YUM!
YUM!

In my line of work, one gets used to eating
when he can and in all sorts of restaurants.
But I enjoy trying different kinds of food.
How's your lunch?" Vulpone asked. Timothy
took one bite and fainted—but before he did
he was heard to mutter: "**One man's meat is
another man's poison**." This means that while
something may be pleasing to one person, it
can be thoroughly unpleasant to another.

165

ONE PICTURE IS WORTH A THOUSAND WORDS

Someone might describe an event or a scene in a thousand words, but a photograph or picture of it could probably tell us as much or more. "Write a summary of the incident and include a couple of photographs," the news editor said. "After all, **one picture is worth a thousand words.**"

166

ONE SWALLOW DOES NOT A SUMMER MAKE

When winter is due to end, migrating birds—like swallows—think of returning to their northern homes. People in the north must be careful, though, for the sight of one swallow doesn't mean winter is really over. That has given us this cautionary advice: don't form hasty opinions or come to quick conclusions on the basis of a few facts or a little information.

ONE'S BARK IS WORSE THAN HIS BITE

You know the situation: you are walking down the street and a dog runs toward you and begins to bark. You are frightened half to death—but then the dog wags his tail and licks your hand. When you've recovered from the shock, you realize the dog's **bark is worse than his bite.** People, too, sometimes "bark," but in time we learn they're not always as frightening as they seem. "Don't let Paul's shouting fool you. **His bark is worse than his bite.**"

OPPORTUNITY ONLY KNOCKS ONCE

Norm was napping under a tree when an apple fell. It bounced and hit a fellow named Newton. Newton became famous writing about gravity, but no one ever heard of Norm. **"Opportunity only knocks once**," Newton smiled, "and Norm slept though it!" This proverb means you should seize an opportunity when it occurs, for it may never occur again.

PADDLE/GO PADDLE ONE'S OWN CANOE

When we **paddle our own canoe**, we direct or control our personal affairs without help from anyone else. This is often used as a command to tell people to stay out of affairs that don't concern them. "When I asked Herbert if he was worried, he told me to **go paddle my own canoe**."

THE PEN IS MIGHTIER THAN THE SWORD

This saying first appeared as a statement in a play about 150 years ago. It means that the written word, either in a book or in the press, is often more powerful and influential than the strength of a great army. Think about this: long after mighty rulers are gone, the literature of their age lives on.

PLAY SECOND FIDDLE

In an orchestra, the person playing what is called 'the first violin' follows the instructions of the conductor and leads the musicians during a performance. A violin is also called a fiddle, so this says anyone who is a follower rather than a leader **plays second fiddle**. "I wasn't happy **playing second fiddle** working for my brother, so I formed my own company," Theodore said.

PLAY WITH FIRE

After seeing jugglers at the circus, Teddy thought it would be fun to learn some of their tricks. Here he is practicing one of them—and if you ask me, he's **playing with fire**. That is, he is taking dangerous risks. "Stop that this minute," his uncle cried. "You could burn the house down!" That made Teddy stop.

POSSESSION IS NINE-TENTHS/POINTS OF THE LAW

In disputes over property ownership, the person in possession of something is sometimes said to have nine-tenths (9/10) a chance of winning it in a legal argument. "Toby found a thousand dollars on the bus. He says it's his because **possession is nine-tenths of the law**. If he's right, then he gets to keep the money."

THE POT CALLING THE
KETTLE BLACK

We use this expression to remind people who criticize others that they may have the same faults. This comes from the fact that cooking pans used over a fire all become black. None is better than the other. "Carol's comments about Martha being messy are an example of **the pot calling the kettle black.**"

POUR OIL ON TROUBLED WATERS

Before the dangers of it to the environment were known, oil was poured on rough seas to calm them. Today this phrase refers to settling disputes or bringing calm to a troubled situation. "This isn't working," Alex said. "Let's see if we can **pour oil on troubled waters** by sitting down and having a quiet talk about it."

PRIDE GOES BEFORE A FALL

This saying from the Bible warns us that having too much confidence, pride or vanity can lead one to an unhappy end. In fact, it happened to Lulu the other day. While walking her dog, a man whistled to warn her of danger. Lulu thought the fellow was admiring her beauty. Now Lulu is in a hospital bed. So is her dog.

PROCRASTINATION IS THE THIEF OF TIME

Procrastination refers to waiting or putting off doing something. Because time moves by quickly, those who procrastinate may miss a valuable opportunity to do or have something. Officer Mutt captured a burglar who fell asleep in a clock shop. "He probably would have gotten away hours earlier if he had realized that **procrastination is the thief of time**," Mutt smiled.

PROMISES ARE
LIKE PIE CRUST

Marry me and I will give you the moon
and the stars and the planets that
encircle us," Cyrano said. "Oh, Cy,
you make me sigh," Roxy replied, "but haven't
you heard that **promises are like pie crust,
made to be broken**?" This proverb, often
shortened to **promises are like pie crust,** says
that many promises cannot be kept. "But I'm
proposing marriage, not running for political
office!" Cyrano said.

THE PROOF OF THE PUDDING IS IN THE EATING

Emily has spent the whole day creating a new dish for dinner. "But **the proof of the pudding is in the eating**," she said, "so I won't know what my family thinks of it until they sit down at the table and try it." What Emily is saying is that the success of something can only be determined when it is put to the test for which it is intended.

PUT A QUART
INTO A PINT POT

I've done it!" Fergus smiled. Fergus thinks he's **put a quart** (of liquid) **into a pint pot**. The expression describes doing something that's impossible. It's used metaphorically, as in this example: "There's no more room," the bus driver said as he closed the doors. "I can't **put a quart in a pint pot,** you know."

PUT ALL ONE'S EGGS IN ONE BASKET

A wise and cautious bird does not **put all her eggs in one basket**," Winifred said. "To do that would be to invite disaster." Those who **put all their eggs in one basket** place all their hopes, money or trust in one plan, scheme or adventure. And that, as Winifred will tell you, is risky!

PUT THE SADDLE ON THE WRONG HORSE

"Hey, are you the person who forgot to lock the stable door last night? All my horses have fled!" Clarence shouted. Horace was astonished. "Of course I locked the stable door. I always lock it. I think you're **putting the saddle on the wrong horse**," he replied. This expression means to blame the wrong person for something. "In that case, I apologize," Clarence said.

183

THE RAIN FALLS ON THE JUST AND THE UNJUST ALIKE

This saying from the Bible (Matthew 5:45) states that no matter how just (good) or unjust (bad) a person is, he must still face the everyday problems that confront us all. **The rain falls on the just and unjust alike,** so being moral and righteous does not necessarily protect a person from the hardships of life. "But I bet Judge Blake had someone around to lend him an umbrella," Albert frowned.

A ROLLING STONE GATHERS NO MOSS

It's true!" Oliver gasped. "**A rolling stone gathers no moss!**" Just as he said that, another stone struck Oliver down. As he was recovering, he reflected on the meaning of this proverb. "I suppose it's said that **a rolling stone gathers no moss** because, like a stone that's always moving, a person who wanders from place to place and job to job has little chance of acquiring property, possessions, or friends."

ROME WAS NOT BUILT IN A DAY

L ong ago, Rome was one of the greatest
and most beautiful cities in the world.
Obviously, it had taken centuries to make
it great, hence this reminder that important
things are not accomplished easily and we
should not expect immediate results from our
work. "It takes time to learn a foreign
language, but be patient and remember that
Rome wasn't built in a day."

RUN WITH THE HARE
AND HUNT WITH
THE HOUNDS

Hares are one thing and hounds are another, and the idea behind this is that one can't be friendly with two opposing or competing groups, teams or factions at the same time. The possibility of disloyalty is implied. "You should cheer for our team or for the visitors, but you're **running with the hare and hunting with the hounds** by cheering for them both!" Herb exclaimed.

THE SANDS (OF TIME) ARE RUNNING OUT

To say **the sands (of time) are running out** is to say that time is passing by quickly—and if a person has something to do he had better do it without delay. "If you hope to pass your examinations, you have little time left to study, Charles. **The sands of time are running out.**"

SEEING IS BELIEVING

This proverb tells us that we can accept something as real or factual only if we can actually see it. **"Seeing is believing,** and I know flying saucers exist because I saw one on my way to work," Ahmed said. Ahmed explained he was commuting via his flying carpet, so if **seeing is believing,** I'll believe Ahmed and his story about flying saucers when I see them both in flight!

189

SHARE AND
SHARE ALIKE

No matter how little money Buddy has, he always shares it. "My mother taught me to **share and share alike**," Buddy said. To **share and share alike** is to share or distribute something equally with someone. It might be something of value, or a job, or a special experience.

SILENCE IS GOLDEN

My kingdom is a noisy place," King Tuttle whispered. "That's the reason I like spending time here in the quiet of my counting room. As you can see, in my kingdom **silence is golden**." King Tuttle is using an old saying that expresses the idea that silence can sometimes be very valuable— maybe even as valuable as gold!

THE SINS OF THE FATHERS ARE/WILL BE VISITED UPON THE CHILDREN

This statement from the Bible (Exodus 20:5) says that people are or will be punished for the wrongs committed by their parents, forefathers, or those who have preceded them. "If we do nothing to clean up our environment, **the sins of the fathers will be visited upon the children** of future generations," the speaker declared.

192

A SKELETON IN THE CLOSET/CUPBOARD

A closely kept secret that, if revealed, would be a source of shame to a person, a family, a group—or even to a country or government—is described as **a skeleton in the closet/cupboard.** "Except for Emma, no one knows that her husband had once been in prison. The secret remains **a skeleton in the closet** and Emma, of course, never talks about it."

A/THE SNAKE
IN THE GRASS

Have you ever known a person who pretends to be your friend, yet at the same time says or does terrible and damaging things behind your back? If so, that person is **a snake in the grass**. "I've just learned that my friend Jane has told the supervisor I'm not qualified for my job, **the snake in the grass!**"

SOMETHING NEW
UNDER THE SUN

When I was a kid, my mother told me I would never be bored, for there would always be **something new under the sun**," Skeet said. As though to prove it, a strange object flew by. This expression says that things are constantly changing and there will always be new and different things happening or created.

195

SPARE THE ROD AND SPOIL THE CHILD

It was once thought that to teach children to behave it was necessary to punish them physically. Only in that way would they grow up to be proper, mature adults. **"Spare the rod and spoil the child,"** parents and teachers declared. Today, of course, punishing a naughty child with a rod or stick is considered abusive, and in enlightened societies is forbidden.

THE SPIRIT IS WILLING, BUT THE FLESH IS WEAK

This saying from the Bible tells us that although we may have a willingness to do something, we frequently fail because of our inner weaknesses. "I planned to paint a portrait of this beautiful steak, but you know how it is: **the spirit is willing, but the flesh is weak,**" Robert said. Well, maybe Robert can paint us a picture of the bone!

A STITCH IN TIME
SAVES NINE

Oh, my! I wish I had remembered that **a stitch in time saves nine** when my panda first needed fixing," Penelope wept. "The poor thing, he's suffered badly." This old saying—often shortened to **a stitch in time**—tells us that by taking immediate action we can prevent a fault, damage or trouble from getting worse.

198

THE STRAW THAT BROKE THE CAMEL'S BACK

If the concerns or responsibilities a person is expected to endure or deal with become too much for him, he may rebel. One more problem could even lead to disaster. Take Omar and his camel, for example. "I know the warnings about **the straw that broke the camel's back**," Omar said, "so I never overload my friendly beast." "I'm not convinced," the camel mumbled as Omar came forward with one more thing to carry.

199

A STRAW WILL SHOW WHICH WAY THE WIND BLOWS

I saw the weathermen on the roof of the observatory preparing a prediction," Lincoln said, "but **a straw will show which way the wind blows**," he smiled. Lincoln's using a metaphor meaning a small incident can reveal an important event. "I saw Don buying a ring. **A straw will show which way the wind blows,** so I guess he's going to ask Polly to marry him."

STRIKE WHILE THE IRON IS HOT

Blacksmiths heat a piece of metal until it is nearly soft. Then, at the right moment, they strike (shape) it into desired forms. That has given us the proverb **strike while the iron is hot**, meaning to act at the right moment to do something to achieve an objective. "I hear that the company is very profitable and the employees are asking for higher pay. Do you suppose they're **striking while the iron is hot?**" Jack asked.

THE SURVIVAL OF THE FITTEST

I seem to remember that it was Charles Darwin who first wrote about **the survival of the fittest**," Grandpa said. "Maybe that's why they want me to climb a mountain to have my blood pressure checked!" This term refers to the idea that only the strongest and most adaptable animals or plants are able to survive.

TAKE THE BULL BY THE HORNS

Roy's a good cowboy but he's going to have to **take the bull by the horns** to capture this bull. "You're kidding!" Roy exclaimed. No, I'm not. I'm just using a proverb that means that one must take firm and positive action to achieve a goal. "In that case I'm going to **take the bull by the horns** and ask the boss for a raise. This is dangerous work!" Roy said.

TEACH AN OLD DOG
NEW TRICKS

There's an old saying that declares it's difficult—possibly impossible—to change someone's ways or habits, especially if he is old and resists change. "I wanted to teach Grandpa how to ice skate, but he said no, you can't **teach an old dog new tricks.**"

TELL TALES OUT OF SCHOOL

I don't understand," Angela said. "Since this refers to telling intimate secrets or revealing information meant to be kept private, I wonder why the word 'school' is included?" "I don't know either, but if you don't want any of our secrets revealed, don't say anything confidential to Kitty. She's been **telling tales out of school** about everyone in the class," Teddy cautioned.

THAT'S WHERE THE
SHOE PINCHES

Timothy and Tina are having a disagreement. "You forgot that today is my birthday," Tina cried. "I didn't forget, I just didn't remember," Timothy answered. "Oh, you don't respect me. **That's where the shoe pinches**," Tina cried. That inspired Timothy to hurry out to get Tina a big bouquet of flowers, for this metaphor means, 'that's the source or cause of a problem or an annoyance.'

THERE ARE NONE SO BLIND AS THOSE WHO WILL NOT SEE

Some people are so stubborn that they refuse to listen to the opinions or ideas of anyone—and they would never admit that they might be wrong about something. They are absolutely unreasonable, and that is what it means when we say **there are none so blind as those who will not see**.

THERE ARE NONE SO DEAF AS THOSE WHO WILL NOT HEAR

One day the boss looked at Wilf and shook his head. "Wilf confirms what I've long suspected: **there are none so deaf as those who will not hear**," he frowned. The boss is using a proverb that says people sometimes hear only what they want to hear.

THERE ARE PLENTY OF OTHER PEBBLES ON THE BEACH

This optimistic expression means there is more of something available or there are more people for one to meet. "I couldn't get into that school, but I'll find another. **There are plenty of other pebbles on the beach.**" "My boyfriend left me, but I don't care. **There are plenty of other pebbles on the beach.**"

THERE ARE TWO SIDES TO EVERY STORY/QUESTION

For years, people have questioned the smile on Mona Lisa's lips. Some say she has a secret, others say she's in love. **"There are two sides to every story,"** the artist said. "Actually, she's thinking about what's for dinner." This expression means that in most matters there can be different ways of looking at things. No single answer is right.

THERE IS A FOOL
BORN EVERY MINUTE

"I have a fascinating job and I see many remarkable things," Nurse Dion said. "But at this moment I can neither confirm nor deny that **there is a fool born every minute**," she smiled. That's good to know, for this saying tells us that there are so many foolish people around that surely one must be born every minute of the day. "Billy thinks that storks distribute babies," Rose interrupted. "On second thought, maybe **there is a fool born every minute**," Nurse Dion laughed.

THERE IS NO FOOL LIKE AN OLD FOOL

"There goes old Prank. He really made me laugh when I was a little kid," Flossie said. Ozzie took a long look. "I guess it's true then, that **there's no fool like an old fool**," he said. This saying tells us that a foolish older person is more shameful than a younger fool.

THERE IS NO ROYAL ROAD TO LEARNING

The road in this proverb isn't truly royal. The term conveys an image of a way that is uncomplicated and can be traveled without effort. "It's true," the Prince pouted, "that **there is no royal road to learning**. I have to study as hard as anyone. The day I become king, though, I intend to change all that!"

213

THERE'S A METHOD IN MY MADNESS

When I've finished this painting, I'll be able to walk in the woods under the boughs of the trees," Robert grinned. "You see, **there's a method in my madness!**" This means that while it might seem that someone is doing something without purpose, he really has a plan in mind—and it will eventually be revealed. "This saying is found in Shakespeare's *Hamlet*," Robert smiled.

THERE'S MORE
THAN ONE WAY
TO SKIN A CAT

"Help! Help! Why did you draw me here in this terrifying situation?" Chadwick cried. "Don't worry. I did it to explain this saying," Ching Yee answered. "Quick! Tell me what it means!" Chadwick pleaded. "Relax. It simply means that there is more than one way of getting a job done," Ching Yee replied. "That makes me feel a lot better," Chadwick sighed, "but would you mind telling the butchers that?"

THERE'S NO PLACE
LIKE HOME

Fergus sat in his rocking chair and surveyed his humble home. "No matter how modest it is, it's the place where I feel most comfortable and at ease," he sighed. I believe Fergus is telling us that **there's no place like home**. "You're right," he replied. "I've traveled all over the world, but **there's no place like home**."

THE THIN END
OF THE WEDGE

It is a known fact," Oliver said, "that something can appear to be small and of no particular importance—yet it can turn out to be the beginning of a major problem. That beginning can be called **the thin end of the wedge**." Oliver paused. "That's because the wedge starts small, but gets bigger."

A THING OF BEAUTY IS A JOY FOREVER

These aren't exotic, they're only wild flowers," Teddy said, "but I've picked them just for you." Angela blushed. "Oh, Teddy, they're beautiful—and there's nothing wild about them. And as the saying goes, **a thing of beauty is a joy forever**." That caused Teddy to blush, for this means that although something beautiful may not last, the happy memory of it will live forever.

THROW THE BABY OUT WITH THE BATH WATER

When reorganizing or changing something, it's important to be careful! Don't be so eager to get rid of the old or the bad that you end up losing the most essential or important things. That's what lies behind this saying. "I restructured the office staff, but in doing so I'm afraid I **threw the baby out with the bath water,** for all my key employees quit!" Bradbury sighed.

TIME AND TIDE WAIT FOR NO MAN

This old saying cautions us that time continues to move on, so if we have things to do, we should not delay. If we do, it may be too late! "If I'm going to make a success of my life, I must begin now. After all, **time and tide wait for no man**," Marlow said.

TIME FLIES

Agatha left a note for Santa: "I've been good all year. Give me a new broom— or else!" Santa left one in Agatha's stocking. "Wow, it's one of those new high-tech models," Agatha said as she tried it out. Weeks later she was still flying high. "It's remarkable how **time flies** when you're having fun!" she giggled. When **time flies,** it goes by so quickly we don't notice it has gone.

TIME HEALS
ALL/OLD WOUNDS

B right Eyes hasn't seen Chadwick in a long time. "We used to be enemies—but I can't remember why," he said. "I suppose that's because **time heals old wounds**," Chadwick replied. This saying tells us that the passing of time helps us to forget things that have caused us pain or made us unhappy. "And led us to have such dreadful fights!" Bright Eyes added.

TIME IS MONEY

No one knows the meaning of this old saying better than my boss. From early morning until late at night, he's busy, busy, busy. **"Time is money,"** he reminds me. **"Time is money."** What he is saying is that time is as precious as money, and a person who wastes time is also wasting money.

THE TIMES CHANGE

WHERE DID THE PEOPLE GO?

Not many things stay the same. Things that we used to think of as being important are often put aside and forgotten as new ones become more worthwhile. New ideas take the place of old ones, and that's why the statement **the times change** is a meaningful one. "Young ladies aren't content to stay at home knitting anymore," Granny sighed. "**The times change**, don't they."

TOO MANY COOKS
SPOIL THE BROTH

The Bobsy brothers are outstanding cooks, and each has his own way of making soup. Therefore, if we turn these three gourmet geniuses loose in the kitchen, they're likely to create confusion and cause trouble, because too many people at work on one project or activity are almost certain to make a mess of it. "That's why it's said that **too many cooks spoil the broth,**" the Bobsy brothers declared.

225

A TROUBLE SHARED IS
A TROUBLE HALVED

I have heard your complaint," Officer Mutt said, "and after taking it up with the management, it has been decided that **a trouble shared is a trouble halved.**" He then made life easier for Albert and his friend. The truth is that **a trouble shared is a trouble halved** refers to discussing one's problems with someone else. "It's supposed to make you feel better," Albert added.

THE TRUTH WILL OUT

Teddy was about to sell some apples when he found that they had worms. "I can't sell these," he said. "It would be dishonest. Besides, with these very alive and very active worms, **the truth will out!**" To say **the truth will out** is to say the truth about something will eventually be discovered or made known.

TURN UP LIKE
A BAD PENNY

Buddy found a penny, but it was bent and looked pretty awful! "I'll make a wish and get rid of it down this well," he decided. A second later, the penny came flying back. "This proves that the proverb is correct," Buddy thought. "The saying **turn up like a bad penny** indicates that something or someone disliked just won't go away."

228

TWO HEADS ARE BETTER THAN ONE

When you have to make an important decision, it's usually best to seek advice, especially from someone friendly. Talking things over with them is better than being unsure or worrying about it alone. When you combine your knowledge with theirs, you'll make a wiser decision. "That's why **two heads are better than one**," Alan said, "and that's why I never make a decision without talking to my wife, Alice."

TWO WRONGS DO NOT MAKE A RIGHT

If a person does something to harm or offend us, that's wrong. If we do something to harm them back, that's wrong too. "So we should remember that one wrong is bad but two wrongs are worse for **two wrongs do not make a right**," Teddy said. "For instance, someone called me names but **two wrongs don't make a right** so I'm not going to complain or criticize him back."

UNEASY IS THE HEAD THAT WEARS THE CROWN

The king has a counting house full of money. "But I also have worries," he said. "There may be mischief afoot in my kingdom, so I must beware!" The he quoted a proverb (from Shakespeare's *Henry IV*): "**Uneasy is the head that wears the crown.**" It means notable or important people are often concerned about losing their positions.

WALLS HAVE EARS

If you have a secret or information that
you'd like to keep private, it's well to take
care how you reveal it to someone. **Walls
have ears**, it is said, and too often our most
intimate conversations have a way of being
overheard. "Don't tell Julie that I saw her
boyfriend with another girl. Remember, the
walls have ears," Agnes whispered.

WASH/HANG ONE'S DIRTY LINEN IN PUBLIC

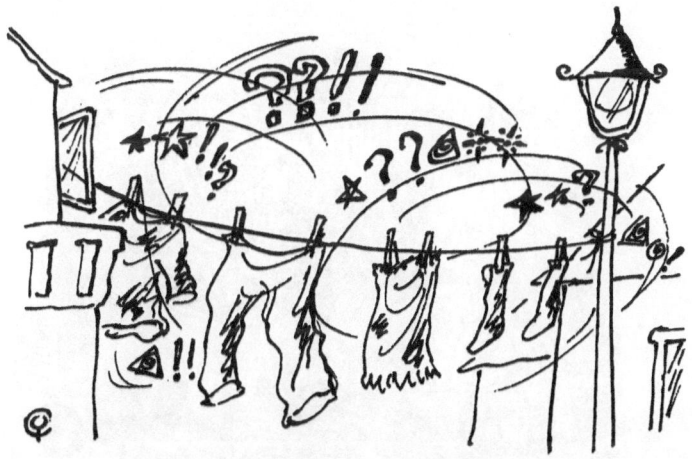

This expression refers to disclosing family problems or private matters to strangers. "My neighbors are constantly arguing in the street. I wish they wouldn't **wash their dirty linen in public**," declared Alice.

WASTE NOT, WANT NOT

L ife is good," Fenwick grinned. "That's
because I practice the old saying **waste
not, want not**. It means if we're careful
and waste nothing we'll never go without
things we need. As you can see," he said
sitting down in his big chair, "it's a life I can
get used to very easily."

A WATCHED POT
NEVER BOILS

Where I come from," Cedric said, "we have a saying that **a watched pot never boils**." The folks who had placed Cedric into their stew pot looked puzzled. "What that means," Cedric continued, "is that if we stand around waiting for something to happen, it seems to take forever and ever. Knowing that, you guys should go away and come back tomorrow!"

THE WAY TO A MAN'S HEART IS THROUGH HIS STOMACH

Most people love to eat. This old proverb suggests that women could win men's adoration if they provided them with a hearty meal. "That may be true," Agnes said. "However, I certainly appreciate Bob's cooking for me as well." Bob smiled and proclaimed, "Let's eat!"

WEAR OUT ONE'S WELCOME

They have a new cook at the place where Albert is staying. "I'm getting fat on this wonderful food," he said to Officer Mutt. "Yes, and you're **wearing out your welcome!**" Mutt replied. When guests **wear out their welcome,** they are no longer welcome, usually because they have stayed on too long and become a nuisance.

WEEP AND YOU WEEP ALONE

Because there is so much that is unhappy in the world, most people prefer to avoid those who are sad and gloomy. "After all," they say, "I have problems of my own!" That's the meaning of this proverb. The complete saying is **laugh and the world laughs with you, weep and you weep alone.**

WHEN IN ROME, DO AS THE ROMANS DO

This old saying (it dates back to the year 370) means that when one visits strangers or a strange place, one should comply with the rules, habits and customs of the people or the place. "I'd like a steak, but everyone here is a vegetarian, so I'll eat what they eat," Peter said. "Like people say, **when in Rome, do as the Romans do.**"

WHEN POVERTY COMES IN THE DOOR, LOVE FLIES OUT THE WINDOW

This has to be one of the saddest remarks I've ever heard," Juliet sighed. "What does it mean?" Romeo asked. "I'll tell you later," she said. While Romeo waits, I can tell you what it says: as soon as a happily married couple begins having financial problems and the bills pile up, their love disappears. Poverty enters their lives and love vanishes.

WHEN THE CAT IS AWAY
THE MICE WILL PLAY

If there's no cat around, mice can do as they
please without worry. "I suppose you think
that humans don't take advantage of
situations when left alone?" Timothy asked.
For example, when Mom and Dad went out,
the children had a party. **When the cat's
away the mice will play,**" Timothy taunted.

WHERE THERE'S MUCK THERE'S BRASS

Muck is dirt and filth. Brass is a slang term for money. This British expression says that although a place or a job is dirty, there is still money to be made there if one doesn't mind the dirt. "I didn't want to live in an industrial area, but it's said **where there's muck there's brass** so I bought a business in one."

WHERE THERE IS A
WILL THERE IS A WAY

H ello, my name is Will. I am without
food or water in an endless desert. But
I see a wishing well ahead. If I put a
coin in it and make a wish, I will be rescued;
for as you may know, **where there's a will
there's a way**." I hope Will's right, for this
saying means if one maintains hope he will
succeed or prevail.

WHICH CAME FIRST, THE CHICKEN OR THE EGG?

This weighty question has perplexed great minds since the beginning of time. It's actually a mystery question, for it can't be answered. We use it when confronted with a paradox or dilemma, and often call it a chicken and egg question. "I don't know which of us arrived here first," Hilton remarked. In fact, no one knows **which came first, the chicken or the egg**.

WHILE THERE IS LIFE
THERE IS HOPE

No matter how bad things are, and no matter how dark the future looks, do not despair! Remember this proverb and know that as long as you are alive, things can—and usually do—improve. "We will inspire each other," Barrymore said to his plant. "We will stay hopeful and be of good cheer knowing that someday we will be found. Remember, **while there is life there is hope!**"

WHO KEEPS COMPANY WITH WOLVES LEARNS TO HOWL

After hearing this proverb, Chadwick went out to see if it was true. "I thoroughly tested it," he said, "and though it may apply to people, it doesn't pertain to cats." **Who keeps company with wolves learns to howl** warns us that if we associate with bad company we, too, will become bad. "Would anyone like to hear me sing?" Chadwick smiled.

A WILLING HORSE

M arsha is **a willing horse**. You know, she hasn't missed a day of work since she began working here," the boss said. Before we go on, I should tell you that Marsha isn't a horse; she's a very nice lady. Her boss called her **a willing horse** because this expression describes someone who does her work well, without ever complaining.

THE WORM TURNS

I'm tired of being pursued by birds," Pedro frowned. "I think it's time **the worm turned.**" Saying that, he struck a bird a mighty blow. When we say **the worm turns,** we are saying that a meek and humble person rebels and stops being meek and humble. In other words, he suddenly asserts himself.

YOU CAN LEAD A HORSE TO WATER, BUT YOU CAN'T MAKE HIM DRINK

There's a saying," Pinky said, "that means we can help, show or encourage someone to do something, but we can't make him do what he is unwilling or unable to do." Pinky is talking about his friend Fred. "I've told him again and again he has to study to graduate but he won't listen. It proves **you can lead a horse to water, but you can't make him drink**," Pinky sighed.

YOU CAN'T HAVE YOUR CAKE AND EAT IT TOO

T here are times when it just isn't possible to have, keep, do or enjoy two things at the same time. Penelope, for example, can't spend her money and still save it for a vacation. She must remember that **you can't have your cake and eat it too**. "But nothing prevents me from taking a photo of my dessert and gazing at it while I'm eating," Penelope smiled.

YOU CAN'T KEEP A GOOD MAN DOWN

I wonder what to do about Albert," Officer Mutt said. "Well, **you can't keep a good man down**," a guard laughed. Mutt was not amused, for the remark refers to a person who shows great determination and refuses to accept defeat. "I suppose I'll have to catch him with my butterfly net," Mutt mumbled.

YOU CAN'T MAKE A
SILK PURSE OUT
OF A SOW'S EAR

A sow is a big pig. Some say its ears look like coin purses. From that we have this old saying that means it's impossible to make something of good quality (like a silk purse) out of poor quality material. By extension, it's not likely a bad person can be changed into a good person. Mother objected to her daughter's boyfriend. **"You can't make a silk purse out of a sow's ear,"** she admonished.

YOU CAN'T MAKE AN OMELETTE WITHOUT BREAKING EGGS

S uch frustration!" Penelope exclaimed.
"Instead of having breakfast, it looks
like I'm going to have a chick farm!
Maybe that's why people say **you can't make
an omelette without breaking eggs!**" The
meaning of this saying is that to achieve a
desired aim, one sometimes must cause
damage, experience difficulties, or
make sacrifices.

YOU CAN'T
GET/SQUEEZE BLOOD
OUT OF A STONE

MAMA DIDN'T TELL US ABOUT MUSEUMS!

A
s we know, stone has no blood.
Therefore, it's pointless to try to
get/squeeze blood out of a stone. The
meaning of this proverb is that you cannot get
something from someone if they don't have it
to give. "Now you tell us," the Mosquito
triplets wept as they left the museum with
bent noses.

YOU NEVER MISS THE WATER UNTIL THE WELL RUNS DRY

Most of the time we don't think about it, but if we were suddenly deprived of water we'd realize the importance of it in our lives. This caution is used as a metaphor for many things that are vital to us. Rupert's girlfriend moved away. "How true it is that **you never miss the water until the well runs dry**," he sighed.

YOU PAYS YOUR MONEY AND YOU TAKES YOUR CHANCES/CHOICE

The nice thing about this saying is that you can say either 'chances' or 'choice,'" Nello said. That's about the only nice thing about it, for it's a humorous way of saying that we sometimes must trust in luck when buying something. "I forgot to mention, I sell horses," Nello said, "and when you buy one from me **you pays your money and you takes your chances.**"

INDEX

Absence Makes The Heart
   Grow Fonder • 1
Actions Speak Louder Than Words • 2
Adam's Ale/Wine • 3
All Roads Lead To Rome • 4
All That Glitters Is Not Gold • 5
All's Fish That Comes To The Net • 6
An Apple A Day Keeps
   the Doctor Away • 7
An Exception To The Rule • 8
An Ounce of Prevention is Better
   Than A Pound of Cure • 9
Another Day, Another Dollar • 10
As A Man Makes His Bed,
   So Must He Lie In It • 11
As I Live and Learn! • 12
Bad Workman Blames His Tools, A • 13
Be On The Safe Side • 14
Beauty Is In The Eye
   Of The Beholder • 15
Beauty Is Only Skin Deep • 16
Bed Of Roses, A • 17
Beggars Can't Be Choosers • 18
Better An Egg Today Than
   A Hen Tomorrow • 19
Better Late Than Never • 20
Big Fish Eat Little Fish • 21
Bird In The Hand Is Worth
   Two In The Bush, (A) • 22
Birds Of A Feather Flock Together • 23
Bite The Hand That Feeds One • 24
Black Sheep, A • 25
Blind Leading The Blind, The • 26
Boys Will Be Boys • 27
Bread Is The Staff Of Life • 28
Buck Stops Here/
   With Someone, The • 29
Burn The Candle At Both Ends • 30
Burnt Child Dreads The Fire, A • 31
Buy A Pig In A Poke • 32
Call A Spade A Spade • 33
Cast Pearls Before Swine • 34
Cat May Look At A King, A • 35
Catch-As-Catch-Can • 36

Catch Your Bear Before
   You Sell Its Skin • 37
Catch/Clutch/Grasp At Straws • 38
Charity Begins At Home • 39
Children Should Be Seen
   And Not Heard • 40
Christmas Comes But
   Once Each Year • 41
Cleanliness Is Next To Godliness • 42
Count Chickens Before
   They Are Hatched • 43
Cry For The Moon • 44
Cry Over Spilled Milk • 45
Curiosity Killed The Cat • 46
Cut Off One's Nose
   To Spite One's Face • 47
Damned If One Does,
   Damned If One Doesn't • 48
Dead Men Tell No Tales • 49
Devil Finds Work For Idle Hands,
   The • 50
Devil Has The Best Tunes, The • 51
Devil Is Not As Black
   As He Is Painted, The • 52
Devil Take The Hindmost, The • 53
Dog Eat Dog • 54
Don't Cry Stinking Fish • 55
Don't Kill The Goose That Laid
   The Golden Eggs • 56
Don't Look A Gift Horse
   In The Mouth • 57
Don't Put The Cart Before
   The Horse • 58
Dose Of One's Own Medicine, A • 59
Draw The Line • 60
Early Bird Catches
   The Worm, The • 61
East Or West, Home Is The Best • 62
Easy Come, Easy Go • 63
Every Cloud Has A Silver Lining • 64
Every Dog Has His Day • 65
Every Law Has A Loophole • 66
Every Picture Tells A Story • 67
Experience Is The Best Teacher • 68

Faint Heart Never Won Fair Lady • 69
Fall Between Two Stools • 70
Fat Is In The Fire, The • 71
Feed A Cold And Starve A Fever • 72
Fiddle While Rome Burns • 73
Fling/Sling/Throw Mud
    At Someone • 74
Flog/Beat A Dead Horse • 75
Fool And His Money Are Soon Parted,
    A • 76
Forgive And Forget • 77
Fresh Fields And Pastures New • 78
Friend In Need Is A Friend Indeed,
    A • 79
Game Is Not Worth The Candle,The • 80
Genius Is An Infinite Capacity
    For Taking Pains • 81
Give Someone Enough Rope
    And He Will Hang Himself • 82
Give The Devil His Due • 83
Gods Send Nuts To Those Who
    Have No Teeth, The • 84
Golden Key Opens Every Door, A • 85
Great Minds Think Alike • 86
Greener Pastures • 87
Grin And Bear It • 88
Half A Loaf Is Better Than None • 89
Half The World Knows Not How The
    Other Half Lives • 90
Harp On One String • 91
Have More Than One String
    To One's Bow • 92
Have Two Bites At The Cherry • 93
He That Sups With The Devil Must Have
    A Long Spoon • 94
He Who Pays The Piper Calls
    The Tunes • 95
Heavy Purse Makes A Light Heart,
    A • 96
Hitch One's Wagon To A Star • 97
Home Is Where The Heart Is • 98
Idle Folk Have The Least Leisure • 99
If It's Not One Thing It's Another • 100
If Money Be Not Thy Servant It
    Will Be Thy Master • 101
If Pigs Could Fly • 102
If The Hat/Shoe Fits, Wear It • 103
If Wishes Were Horses,
    Beggars Would Ride • 104

If You Can't Bite, Don't Show Your Teeth
    • 105
If You Can't Lick Them, Join Them • 106
If You Scratch My Back,
    I'll Scratch Yours • 107
In For A Penny, In For A Dollar/Pound •
    108
In The Land Of The Blind, The
    One-Eyed Man Is King • 109
It Shouldn't Happen To A Dog • 110
It Takes A Thief To Catch A Thief • 111
It Takes Two To Make A Quarrel • 112
It's A Small World • 113
It's Love That Makes The World Go
    'Round/Around • 114
Jam Tomorrow • 115
Job Worth Doing Is A Job
    Worth Doing Well, A • 116
Keep A Dog And Bark Oneself • 117
Keep The Wolf From The Door • 118
Kill Two Birds With One Stone • 119
Know A Hawk From A Handsaw • 120
Laugh And The World Laughs
    With You • 121
Laughter Is The Best Medicine • 122
Least Said, Soonest Forgotten • 123
Leave/Let Well Enough Alone • 124
Leopard Can't Change His Spots, A • 125
Let Sleeping Dogs Lie • 126
Life Is Just A Bowl Of Cherries • 127
Light Not A Candle To The Sun • 128
Lightning Never Strikes Twice • 129
Like A Bull In A China Shop • 130
Like Looking For A Needle
    In A Haystack • 131
Little Pitchers Have Big Ears • 132
Lock The Stable Door After The
    Horse Has Bolted • 133
Longest Day Must Have An End,
    The • 134
Look Before You Leap • 135
Look On The Bright/Sunny Side • 136
Losers Weepers, Finders Keepers • 137
Love Is Blind • 138
Love Me, Love My Dog • 139
Make Hay While The Sun Shines • 140
Make A Mountain Out
    Of A Molehill • 141
Man Does Not Live By Bread Alone • 142

Manners Make The Man • 143
Many Hands Make Light Work • 144
March Comes In Like A Lion And Goes
    Out Like A Lamb • 145
Marriages Are Made In Heaven • 146
Might As Well Be Hung For A Sheep
    As A Lamb • 147
Money Burns A Hole In
    Someone's Pocket • 148
Money Can't Buy Everything • 149
Money Doesn't Grow On Trees • 150
Money Is The Root Of All Evil • 151
Money Talks • 152
Mountain Isn't Going To Come
    To Mohammed, The • 153
Mountain Labors And Brings
    Forth A Mouse, The • 154
My Home Is My Castle • 155
Necessity Is The Mother Of Invention •
    156
Never Say Die • 157
New Broom Sweeps Clean, A • 158
No News Is Good News • 159
Not For All The Coffee In Brazil • 160
Not For All The Tea In China • 161
Not The Only Pebble On The Beach •
    162
On A/One's High Horse • 163
Once Bitten, Twice Shy • 164
One Man's Meat Is Another
    Man's Poison • 165
One Picture Is Worth A Thousand Words
    • 166
One Swallow Does Not A
    Summer Make • 167
One's Bark Is Worse Than His Bite • 168
Opportunity Only Knocks Once • 169
Paddle/Go Paddle One's Own Canoe •
    170
Pen Is Mightier Than The Sword, The •
    171
Play Second Fiddle • 172
Play With Fire • 173
Possession Is Nine-Tenths/Points
    Of The Law • 174
Pot Calling The Kettle Black, The • 175
Pour Oil On Troubled Waters • 176
Pride Goes Before A Fall • 177
Procrastination Is The Thief Of Time •
    178

Promises Are Like Pie Crust • 179
Proof Of The Pudding Is In The Eating •
    180
Put A Quart Into A Pint Pot • 181
Put All One's Eggs In One Basket • 182
Put The Saddle On The Wrong Horse •
    183
Rain Falls On The Just And
    The Unjust Alike, The • 184
Rolling Stone Gathers No Moss, A • 185
Rome Was Not Built In A Day • 186
Run With The Hare And Hunt
    With The Hounds • 187
Sands (Of Time) Are Running Out, The •
    188
Seeing Is Believing • 189
Share And Share Alike • 190
Silence Is Golden • 191
Sins Of The Fathers Are/Will Be Visited
    Upon The Children • 192
Skeleton In The Closet/Cupboard, A •
    193
Snake In The Grass, A/The • 194
Something New Under The Sun • 195
Spare The Rod And Spoil The Child
    • 196
Spirit Is Willing, But The Flesh Is Weak,
    The • 197
Stitch In Time Saves Nine, A • 198
Straw That Broke The Camel's Back, The
    • 199
Straw Will Show Which Way The Wind
    Blows, A • 200
Strike While The Iron Is Hot • 201
Survival Of The Fittest, The • 202
Take The Bull By The Horns • 203
Teach An Old Dog New Tricks • 204
Tell Tales Out Of School • 205
That's Where The Shoe Pinches • 206
There Are None So Blind As Those Who
    Will Not See • 207
There Are None So Deaf As Those Who
    Will Not Hear • 208
There Are Plenty Of Other Pebbles
    On The Beach • 209
There Are Two Sides To Every
    Story/Question • 210
There Is A Fool Born Every Minute • 211
There Is No Fool Like An Old Fool • 212

There Is No Royal Road
To Learning • 213
There's A Method In My Madness • 214
There's More Than One Way
To Skin A Cat • 215
There's No Place Like Home • 216
The Thin End Of The Wedge • 217
Thing Of Beauty Is A Joy
Forever, A • 218
Throw The Baby Out With
The Bath Water • 219
Time And Tide Wait For No Man • 220
Time Flies • 221
Time Heals All/Old Wounds • 222
Time Is Money • 223
Times Change, The • 224
Too Many Cooks Spoil The Broth • 225
Trouble Shared Is A Trouble Halved,
A • 226
Truth Will Out, The • 227
Turn Up Like A Bad Penny • 228
Two Heads Are Better Than One • 229
Two Wrongs Do Not Make A Right • 230
Uneasy Is The Head That Wears
The Crown • 231
Walls Have Ears • 232
Wash/Hang One's Dirty Linen
In Public • 233
Waste Not, Want Not • 234
Watched Pot Never Boils, A • 235
Way To A Man's Heart Is
Through His Stomach, The • 236
Wear Out One's Welcome • 237
Weep And You Weep Alone • 238
When In Rome, Do As The
Romans Do • 239
When Poverty Comes In The Door, Love
Flies Out The Window • 240
When The Cat Is Away,
The Mice Will Play • 241
Where There's Muck There's Brass • 242
Where There Is A Will
There Is A Way • 243
Which Came First, The Chicken
Or The Egg? • 244
While There Is Life There Is Hope • 245
Who Keeps Company With Wolves
Learns To Howl • 246
Willing Horse, A • 247
Worm Turns, The • 248

You Can Lead A Horse To Water,
But You Can't Make Him Drink • 249
You Can't Have Your Cake
And Eat It Too • 250
You Can't Keep A Good Man Down •
251
You Can't Make A Silk Purse
Out Of A Sow's Ear • 252
You Can't Make An Omelette
Without Breaking Eggs • 253
You Can't Get/Squeeze Blood
Out Of A Stone • 254
You Never Miss The Water Until
The Well Runs Dry • 255
You Pays Your Money And You
Takes Your Chances/Choice • 256

www.idiom-magic.com

978-0-595-35079-7
0-595-35079-8